What Are Light Waves?

Robin Johnson

Crabtree Publishing Company
www.crabtreebooks.com

Author
Robin Johnson

Publishing plan research and development
Reagan Miller

Editorial director
Kathy Middleton

Editor
Kathy Middleton

Proofreader
Shannon Welbourn

Design
Samara Parent

Photo research
Samara Parent

**Production coordinator
and prepress technician**
Samara Parent

Print coordinator
Margaret Amy Salter

Photographs
Thinkstock: pages 8, 10
Kobby Dagan / Shutterstock.com: page 6
testing / Shutterstock.com: page 9
All other images by Shutterstock

Library and Archives Canada Cataloguing in Publication

Johnson, Robin (Robin R.), author
    What are light waves? / Robin Johnson.

(Light and sound waves close-up)
Includes index.
Issued in print and electronic formats.
ISBN 978-0-7787-0519-2 (bound).--ISBN 978-0-7787-0523-9 (pbk.).--
ISBN 978-1-4271-9008-6 (html).--ISBN 978-1-4271-9012-3 (pdf)

    1. Light--Wave-length--Juvenile literature. 2. Wave theory of
light--Juvenile literature. I. Title.

QC455.J64 2014   j535   C2014-900807-4
                                      C2014-900808-2

Library of Congress Cataloging-in-Publication Data

CIP available at Library of Congress

Crabtree Publishing Company

www.crabtreebooks.com   1-800-387-7650

Printed in the USA/112015/SN20150910

Published in Canada
Crabtree Publishing
616 Welland Ave.
St. Catharines, Ontario
L2M 5V6

Published in the United States
Crabtree Publishing
PMB 59051
350 Fifth Avenue, 59th Floor
New York, New York 10118

Published in the United Kingdom
Crabtree Publishing
Maritime House
Basin Road North, Hove
BN41 1WR

Published in Australia
Crabtree Publishing
3 Charles Street
Coburg North
VIC 3058

Contents

What is light?

Light is the brightness that lets you see the world around you. It shines down from the sun when you ride your bike. Light **glows** from your campfire when you roast marshmallows. It shines from a lamp when you are reading a bedtime story.

See the light!

Light is everywhere! Some lights are very bright. The sun is the brightest light. Others are **dim**. Dim means not bright. A night-light gives off only a little light. Some lights flash or blink on and off. Others are different colors. There are all kinds of lights. Look around you. What lights do you see? How do they look?

firefly

Fireflies are insects that glow.
To glow means to give off light.

We need light

Light is very important. It helps you see all the things you need to do. When you want to eat a snack at night, you turn on the kitchen light. You open the fridge and a light comes on inside it. Without light, you might reach for the cookie jar, but grab a jar of pickles instead!

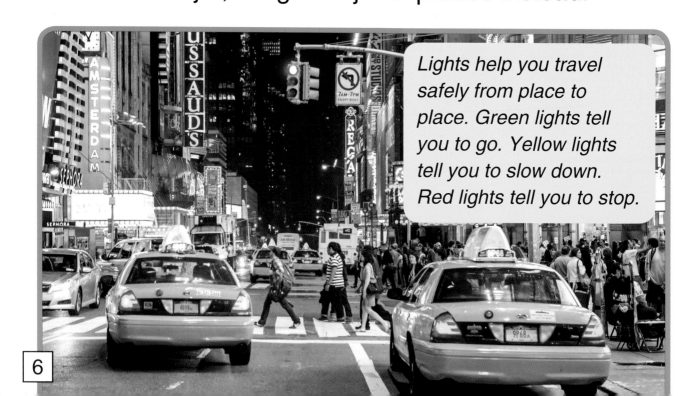

Lights help you travel safely from place to place. Green lights tell you to go. Yellow lights tell you to slow down. Red lights tell you to stop.

Guiding light

Light also helps you **communicate**. To communicate is to share ideas and information. Lighthouses use light to communicate with ships. A lighthouse is a tower with a large lamp at the top. It shines brightly to warn ships sailing along the coast that they are close to shore.

What do you think?

Name some lights in different places you use every day. How do they help you?

In the dark

When the sun goes down each day, everything is in darkness. You cannot see when there is no light. Sometimes the moon is bright enough to help you find your way. Inside caves and other dark places, you can carry a flashlight to light your way.

A campfire and a lantern give off light to help you see at night on a camping trip.

Streetlights and lights on cars help drivers see when driving at night.

Out like a light

Sometimes the power goes out when there is a bad storm. Suddenly all the lights in your home go off! Your parents hurry to get candles and flashlights. The lights help you see in the dark.

What do you think?

Turn off all the lights. Close the curtains. Is the room dark? Is it harder to see now than it was before? Why?

Light is energy

Light is a form of **energy**. Energy is the power to do work. There are many forms of energy. We use some forms of energy to heat our homes. We use other forms of energy to fuel our bodies.

Over a hundred years ago, people used candles to light their homes. Today, we use electricity instead. Electricity allows us to light up any room with the flip of a light switch.

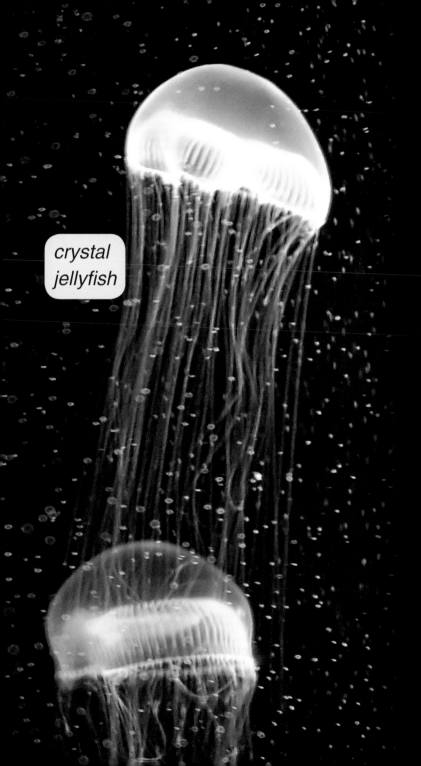

crystal jellyfish

See in the sea

Some sea creatures use energy to make their own light! They live deep in the ocean where it is very dark. The animals glow to communicate with other animals. They also use light to draw the curious animals near. Then they catch them for dinner!

The sun

The sun is our main **source** of light. A source is the place where something comes from. The sun is like a giant light bulb in the sky! It is very powerful. It shines light on the whole world.

The sun is so hot and bright, it can actually hurt you! You should put sunscreen on your skin so the sun will not burn it. You should also wear a hat and sunglasses to protect your eyes.

What do you think?

What activities can you do during the day that you cannot do at night? What activities need light from the sun?

The sun gives us light and warmth, even on cloudy days!

Everything under the sun

The sun also heats Earth. It keeps all living things warm. Without the sun, the world would be very dark and cold. People or animals could not live here. No flowers or other plants could grow. We need the sun to keep Earth warm and bright.

Light waves

The sun, light bulbs, and all other sources of light make light waves. **Light waves** are rays, or beams of energy, that you can see with your eyes. Your eye sees different light waves as different colors.

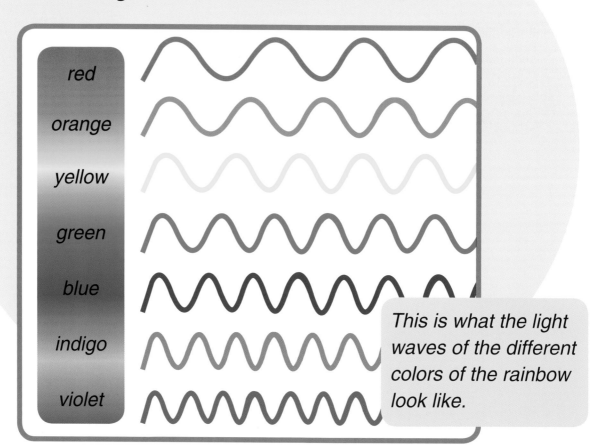

red

orange

yellow

green

blue

indigo

violet

This is what the light waves of the different colors of the rainbow look like.

Long and short

Light waves are different lengths. Some light waves are long. Other light waves are short. Different size light waves make different colors. What is your favorite color?

When sunlight hits raindrops in just the right way, we can see all of light's colors in the form of a rainbow.

A light matter

Light waves travel from their source in straight lines. The waves are straight until they meet up with **matter**. Matter is anything that takes up space and that you can see or touch. Everything is made up of matter. Your toys are made of matter. This book is made of matter. You are made of matter, too!

What is the matter? Find all the matter in this picture!

Bounce around

When light waves meet an object, the object's matter **reflects** the light. To reflect means to bounce off something. The light waves change direction and keep going. They keep moving and bouncing off other objects in their path.

What do you think?

Think of this lamp as the sun and the ball as the moon. Is the sun or the moon the source of light? Why does the moon look to us like it is glowing?

light wave

reflected light

Eyes see the world

Our eyes catch light waves as they move and bounce from place to place. Light enters the eye through the **pupil**. The pupil is the black spot in the center of your eye. It is a hole that grows or shrinks to let in more or less light.

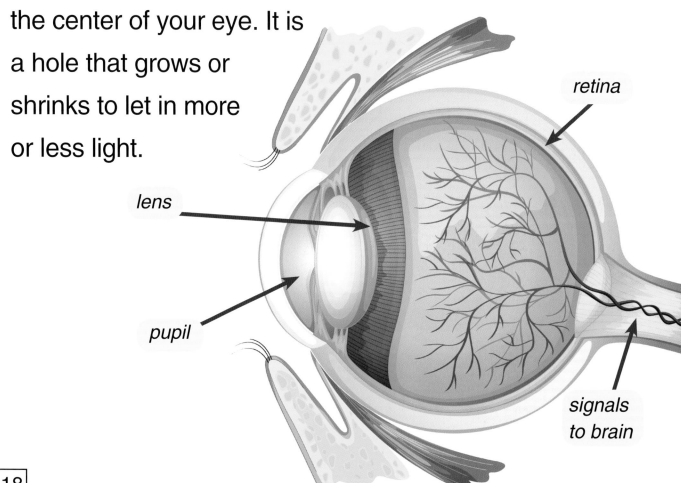

retina

lens

pupil

signals to brain

Clear signals

After entering your eye, the light waves hit the **lens**. The lens **focuses** the light. To focus is to make clear. The light continues on and hits the **retina** at the back of your eye. The retina sends signals to your brain. Your brain makes sense of all the amazing things you see!

If the lenses in your eyes do not work well, you cannot see clearly. Then you need to get glasses that will correct the way your eyes see.

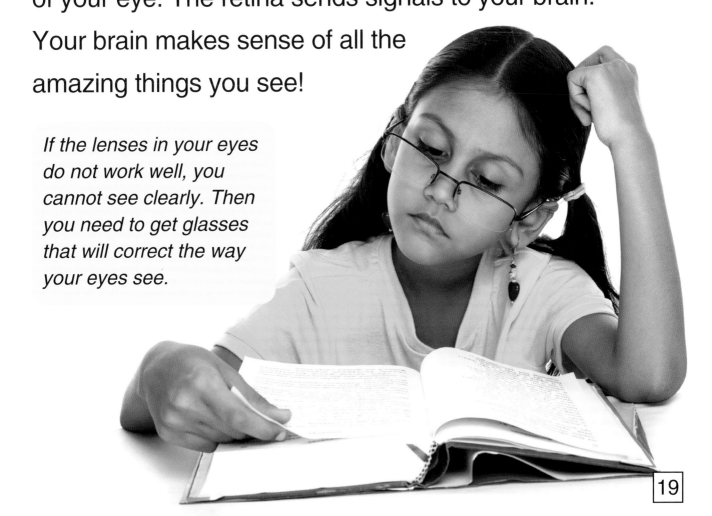

I spy with my little eye

How important is light? Follow these steps to make a pinhole box. Then spy with your little eye and see what you can see. Do not be afraid of the dark!

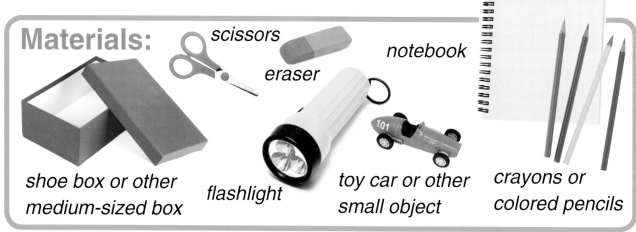

Materials:

scissors

eraser

notebook

shoe box or other medium-sized box

flashlight

toy car or other small object

crayons or colored pencils

What to do:

1. Carefully cut a tiny hole in the lid of the box.

2. Put an eraser or other small object inside the box. Close the lid.

3. Look into the hole in the box. Write down or draw what you see in your notebook.

4. Shine a flashlight into the hole. Write down what you see now.

5. Open the lid and look inside the box. Can you see the object? Draw it.

Think outside the box

When you looked into the box without light, could you see inside? No! It was dark. You cannot see in the dark. When you put light into the box, could you see inside? Yes! Light lets you see inside and outside. It lets you see up and down and all around. Light lets you see it all!

What do you think?

What would happen if you made a bigger hole in the box? How would it change what you could see inside?

Learning more

Books

Flash!: Light and How We See Things by Peter Riley. Franklin Watts Ltd., 2008.

Light by Claire Llewellyn. Franklin Watts Ltd., 2008.

Light & Sound: The Best Start in Science by Clint Twist. Ticktock Books, 2009.

Light Is All Around Us by Wendy Pfeffer. *HarperCollins, 2014.*

What Is Sight? by Molly Aloian. Crabtree Publishing Company, 2013.

What Are Shadows and Reflections? by Robin Johnson. Crabtree Publishing Company, 2014.

Websites

BBC Bitesize: Light
www.bbc.co.uk/bitesize/ks2/science/physical_processes/light/read/1/

Kids Health: Your Eyes
http://kidshealth.org/kid/htbw/eyes.html

Science Kids: Light for Kids
www.sciencekids.co.nz/light.html

Words to know

communicate (kuh-MYOO-ni-keyt) *verb* To share ideas and information

dim *adjective* Not bright

energy (EN-er-jee) *noun* The power to do work

focus (FOH-kuh s) *verb* To make clear

glow (gloh) *verb* To give off light

lens (lenz) *noun* The part of the eye that focuses light to make clear pictures

light wave (lahyt weyv) *noun* A ray of energy you see with your eyes

matter (MAT-er) *noun* Something that takes up space

pupil (PYOO-puh l) *noun* The black spot in the center of the eye that controls how much light enters it

reflect (ri-FLEKT) *verb* To bounce off something

retina (RET-n-uh) *noun* The part of the eye that gets pictures and sends them to the brain

source (sohrs) *noun* The place where something begins or comes from

A *noun* is a person, place, or thing.
An *adjective* is a word that tells you what something is like.
A *verb* is an action word that tells you what someone or something does.

Index